The Hare and the Tortoise

Retold and dramatised from the
Aesop's fable as a reading play
for partners or small groups.

Ellie Hallett

Ways to read this story

This story is suitable for school and home. Some 'how to read' ideas are below.

- With a partner or small group, take it in turns to read the rows.

- Don't rush! This helps you to say each word clearly.

- Think of yourselves as actors by adding lots of facial and vocal expression. Small gaps of silence also create dramatic energy. These techniques will bring the story to life.

- If you meet a new word, try to break it down and then say it again. If you have any problems, ask your teacher or a reading buddy.

- Don't be scared of unusual words. They will become your new best friends.
  (New words strengthen your general knowledge and enable you to become vocabulary-rich in your day-to-day life.)

Have fun!

Arthur Rackman   1912

'Hello Hare!'

'Hello, Tortoise!'

'Lovely day for a walk!'

'Yes it is, but I need to ask you a quick question, Tortoise.'

'Fire away, Hare.'

'Don't you find it a terrible bore to be so slow?'

'I beg your pardon! What did you say?'

'I asked you if you found it really boring to be so slow.'

'Ahem. Mmmm.
Well, I like being slow because it gives me time to look at things as I move along.'

'Well, I couldn't stand it, ambling along with my house on my back. I prefer to arrive sooner rather than later.'

'There are advantages in being slow, especially if there is danger.'

'Yes, yes, but plod, plod plodding is your only choice.'

'So what's your problem, Hare?'

'The problem is that you can't ever be quick. I can be slow or fast.

It's all about having long strong legs.'

'My legs are also quite str ...'

'I can stroll, saunter and sprint.'

'But my ...'

'And I can lope, dash and leap.'

'Very good, Hare, yes, very good. But let me tell you about an idea that has just leapt into my head.'

'And I can dart and scoot and scamper ... What did you say?'

'I said I have an idea.'

'An idea is not much use if it just stays in your head, Tortoise, old boy.

So what's this great idea of yours, huh?'

'How about we have a race to see who ...'

'A race, old chum? Did you say a **race**? Ha ha ha. I've never ...'

'Yes, a race.

It will help us know once and for all who is the faster of the two – a hare or a tortoise.'

'Ha! Ha! You are a brave chap, if I may say so, Tortoise. Ha ha!'

'A Hare and Tortoise race will ...'

'And you want to be in a race, a slow and panting old tortoise?'

'... we'll need a Race Judge to set the course, start us off and ...'

'... me the super-fit, super-fast king-of-the-road Hare?'

... then be at the finishing line to announce the winner.'

'This will be a walk-over for quick little me, Tortoise. Too easy!'

'Whatever.'

'Hmmm ... But who around here would be a suitable race referee?'

'I think our answer is about to arrive from another story.'

'And who might that be on this fine morning?'

'Good morning, Fox, and such a perfect day! Are you well?'

'Good morning, Tortoise and Hare. I'm perfectly well, thank you.

I trust you are both in the peak of good health?'

Illustration 'The Fox and the Grapes' by Calvert-Rogniat (1812 - 1875)

'We certainly are, which leads us to asking if we could impose on your time to be our Race Judge.'

'A judge, huh.

My pleasure entirely. I can't say I have ever been a Race Judge before. And what would be my duties in this esteemed role?'

'We'd be honoured if you could set the course and be our time-keeper.'

'Why certainly. It will be indeed a pleasure. More than happy to be of assistance.'

'Time for the race of your life, Tortoise, old bean, ready or not.'

'I am more than ready, Tortoise. Over to you, Judge Fox.'

'Here are my instructions. The start and finish line will be here.'

'And then what, Foxy Legs?'

'... ahem ... Over the bridge, through the forest and back over the bridge to this spot.'

'Let me get this straight, Tortoise and Foxy, because I intend to win. So it's bridge, forest, bridge, here.'

'That's exactly right. Prepare yourselves.

Now, on your marks.

Get ready. Get set.

Go!'

'Ha ha! See you soon!

Over the bridge I fly!

I'm sprinting faster than a Jack Rabbit being chased by a bumble bee!'

'Ah. Peace and quiet at last!

The only way to stop that show-off Hare talking about himself was to have a race.'

'Already I am in the forest, and Tortoise is, of course, far behind. Hmmm.

Whoa! What have we here? These strawberries look rather delicious.'

'Over the bridge and down the other side on my short legs.
The forest is just around the corner, so I'm making rather good time.'

From *The Baby's Own Aesop* - Walter Crane (1908 – 1952)

'That strawberry snack was excellent.

Now it's nap time. Ha ha! My super-fast legs will beat that old slow-coach Tortoise any day.

No worries!'

'And into the forest I go. But who's that resting under that tree?

Oh my goodness! It's Hare, and, I think he's fast asleep.'

'Snore, snore.'

'I may be slow, but I'll just keep plodding along one step at a time.'

'Hmmm ...

I may as well snooze a bit longer before I win the race.'

'Ah yes!

And there's Judge Fox up ahead waiting for us at the finish line.

I think he may be more than a little surprised to see me heading for the finish line!'

'My goodness! I had better get a move on. Now I wonder how far back Tortoise is ...'

'Almost there. But will I make it?'

'A quick sprint should do the trick.

I'll pass Tortoise with time to spare

and then leap over the finish line.'

'At last! I've made it, even carrying

my house with me all the way!'

Printed with permission, Lehman College Art Gallery,
The City University NY

'Oh hello, Hare. As Race Judge, I am proud to congratulate Tortoise on his magnificent effort in ...'

'You're joking! How is this possible? I am much faster ... '

'... not only completing the course, but winning the race fair and square and if I may say so, in as fine a style as one could hope to witness.'

'But how can old stumpy-legs Tortoise beat me?

I am a champion runner with long legs purpose-built for speed.'

'I know my legs are short and stumpy.

But, well, even if I say so myself, these little stumps did the job.'

'And as Race Judge –

I proudly and officially announce –

that the winner of this race –

is none other than –

the magnificent –

the one and only ...

Mr Tortoise!'

'As runner-up, I hate to admit it, but congratulations, Tortoise.

You have shown not just me, but the whole wide world that ... '

(said together by all readers) **'Slow and steady wins the race!'**

Illustration by Calvet-Rogniat (1812 – 1875)

Illustration by Felix Lorioux (1872 – 1964)

From *Fables de La Fontaine*

Milo Winter (1888 – 1956)

The Readers' Theatre series by *Ellie Hallett*

These **Readers' Theatre** stories have a major advantage in that everyone has equal reading time. Best of all, they are theatrical, immediately engaging and entertaining. Ellie Hallett's unique play-in-rows format, developed and trialled with great success in her own classrooms, combines expressive oral reading, active listening, peer teaching, vocabulary building, visualisation, and best of all, enjoyment.

ISBN	Title	Author	Price	E-book Price	QTY
9781921016455	Goldilocks and The Three Bears	Hallett, Ellie	9.95	9.95	
9781925398045	Jack and the Beanstalk	Hallett, Ellie	9.95	9.95	
9781925398069	The Fox and the Goat	Hallett, Ellie	9.95	9.95	
9781925398076	The Gingerbread Man	Hallett, Ellie	9.95	9.95	
9781925398052	Little Red Riding Hood and the Five Senses	Hallett, Ellie	9.95	9.95	
9781925398083	The Town Mouse and the Country Mouse	Hallett, Ellie	9.95	9.95	
9781925398014	The Two Travellers	Hallett, Ellie	9.95	9.95	
9781925398007	The Enormous Turnip	Hallett, Ellie	9.95	9.95	
9781925398090	The Hare and the Tortoise	Hallett, Ellie	9.95	9.95	
9781925398106	The Wind and the Sun	Hallett, Ellie	9.95	9.95	
9781925398113	The Three Wishes	Hallett, Ellie	9.95	9.95	
9781921016554	The Man, the Boy and the Donkey	Hallett, Ellie	9.95	9.95	
9781925398120	The Fox and the Crow	Hallett, Ellie	9.95	9.95	
9781920824921	Who Will Bell the Cat?	Hallett, Ellie	9.95	9.95	
9781925398021	The Ugly Duckling	Hallett, Ellie	9.95	9.95	

KNOWLEDGE
BOOKS AND SOFTWARE
PUBLISHING

www.kbs.com.au

Readers' Theatre